# AIR FRYER RECIPES
## FOR BEGINNERS

*Losing Weight and Staying in Shape is
Very Easy with Air Fryer Recipes*

## SAM HAMIL

# Table of Contents

## Sommario

# Introduction

## What is an air fryer?

It is an appliance that typically has an egg shape, more or less square, with a removable basket in which you put the food to be cooked. It takes advantage of the concept of air cooking at high temperatures that reach up to 200° allowing a healthy "frying-not-frying" of fresh food. Abandon, then, the thought of frying in which the food is immersed in a lot of oil because the amount of oil used inside the air fryer can be as little as a couple of teaspoons of spray. True frying in lots of hot oil is practically "dangerous", especially in case you abuse it or don't pay proper attention. In the air fryer, the oil will never reach the smoke point and is therefore not harmful.

The hot air, which reaches high temperatures, circulates in the compartment of the air fryer allowing even cooking of food both outside and inside. This way you can cook meat, fish, vegetables and thousands of other dishes in no time - in short, you can prepare many recipes with the air fryer. Meat cooked in the air fryer is succulent, tender, and soft, excess fat runs off and does not remain inside the meat giving it an exceptional flavor.

# The air fryer also works as an oven and grill…

The air fryer is very different and in addition to its main purpose, the air cooking of food for a light and healthy fried, it is also an appliance that serves as an oven for gratin for different recipes, pasta dishes, vegetables, to prepare cakes and pies of all kinds, muffins, buns, pizzas. It has been shown that in the best performing models, the air fryer allows eliminating excess fat, even up to 50%, without altering the flavor of food, giving the right friability typical of fried foods.

# Which air fryer to choose to buy?

For air fryer selection, the suggestion could also be a reliable product to urge better and better results. A high-quality product makes an equivalent quality product. Therefore, it would be fair to consider spending a bit more on a much better-performing air fryer that also has better quality materials. However, depending on your needs, many excellent products are affordable.

Now you just need to take a look at the air fryer recipes. They are all proven, safe and outstanding recipes!

# Chicken

# Chicken Drumsticks with Blue Cheese Sauce

*(Ready in about 25 minutes | Servings 4)*

246 Calories; 20g Fat; 1.5g Carbs; 14.2g Protein; 0.2g Sugars

## Ingredients

1/2 teaspoon shallot powder
1/2 teaspoon garlic powder
1/2 teaspoon coriander
1/4 teaspoon red pepper flakes
Sea salt and ground black pepper, to season
2 chicken drumsticks, skinless and boneless
1/4 cup blue cheese, softened
4 tablespoons mayonnaise
4 tablespoons sour cream
1 teaspoon fresh garlic, pressed
1 teaspoon fresh lime juice

## Directions

In a resealable bag, place the shallot powder, garlic powder, coriander, red pepper, salt and black pepper; add in the chicken drumsticks and shake until they are well coated.
Spritz the chicken drumsticks with a nonstick cooking oil and place in the cooking basket.
Air fry the chicken drumsticks at 370 degrees F for 20 minutes, turning them over halfway through the cooking time.
Meanwhile, make the sauce by whisking the remaining ingredients.
Place the sauce in your refrigerator until ready to serve.
Serve the chicken drumsticks with blue cheese sauce. Bon appétit!

# Meatballs with Cheese

*(Ready in about 15 minutes | Servings 4)*

497 Calories; 24g Fat; 20.7g Carbs; 41.9g Protein; 4.1g Sugars

## Ingredients

1 pound ground turkey
1/2 pound ground pork
1 egg, well beaten
1 cup seasoned breadcrumbs
1 teaspoon dried basil
1 teaspoon dried rosemary
1/4 cup Manchego cheese, grated
2 tablespoons yellow onions, finely chopped
1 teaspoon fresh garlic, finely chopped
Sea salt and ground black pepper, to taste

## Directions

In a mixing bowl, combine all the ingredients until everything is well incorporated.
Shape the mixture into 1-inch balls.
Cook the meatballs in the preheated Air Fryer at 380 degrees for 7 minutes. Shake halfway through the cooking time. Work in batches.
Serve with your favorite pasta. Bon appétit!

# Turkey Wings with Roasted Potatoes

*(Ready in about 55 minutes | Servings 4)*

567 Calories; 14.3g Fat; 65.7g Carbs; 46.1g Protein; 2.9g Sugars

## Ingredients

4 large-sized potatoes, peeled and cut into 1-inch chunks

1 tablespoon butter, melted

1 teaspoon rosemary

1 teaspoon garlic salt

1/2 teaspoon ground black pepper

1 ½ pounds turkey wings

2 tablespoons olive oil

2 garlic cloves, minced

1 tablespoon Dijon mustard

1/2 teaspoon cayenne pepper

## Directions

Add the potatoes, butter, rosemary, salt, and pepper to the cooking basket.

Cook at 400 degrees F for 12 minutes. Reserve the potatoes, keeping them warm.

Now, place the turkey wings in the cooking basket that is previously cleaned and greased with olive oil. Add the garlic, mustard, and cayenne pepper.

Cook in the preheated Air Fryer at 350 degrees f for 25 minutes.

Turn them over and cook an additional 15 minutes.

Test for doneness with a meat thermometer. Serve with warm potatoes.

# Chicken and Cheese Stuffed Mushrooms

*(Ready in about 15 minutes | Servings 4)*

166 Calories; 8.2g Fat; 3.4g Carbs; 19.1g Protein; 2.3g Sugars

## Ingredients

9 medium-sized button mushrooms, cleaned and steams removed
1/2 pound chicken white meat, ground
2 ounces goat cheese, room temperature
2 ounces cheddar cheese, grated
1 teaspoon soy sauce
2 tablespoons scallions, finely chopped
1 teaspoon fresh garlic, finely chopped
Sea salt and red pepper, to season

## Directions

Pat the mushrooms dry and set them aside.
Thoroughly combine all ingredients, except for the cheddar cheese, in a mixing bowl. Stir to combine well and stuff your mushrooms. Bake in your Air Fryer at 370 degrees F for 5 minutes. Top with cheddar cheese and continue to cook an additional 3 to 4 minutes or until the cheese melts. Bon appétit!

# Turkey Sandwiches

*(Ready in about 45 minutes | Servings 4)*

427 Calories; 18g Fat; 33.5g Carbs; 32.8g Protein; 6.1g Sugars

## Ingredients

1 pound turkey tenderloins
1 tablespoon Dijon-style mustard
1 tablespoon olive oil
Sea salt and ground black pepper, to taste
1 teaspoon Italian seasoning mix
1/4 cup all-purpose flour
1 cup turkey stock
8 slices sourdough, toasted
4 tablespoons tomato ketchup
4 tablespoons mayonnaise
4 pickles, sliced

## Directions

Rub the turkey tenderloins with the mustard and olive oil. Season with salt, black pepper, and Italian seasoning mix.
Cook the turkey tenderloins at 350 degrees F for 30 minutes, flipping them over halfway through. Let them rest for 5 to 7 minutes before slicing. For the gravy, in a saucepan, place the drippings from the roasted turkey. Add 1/8 cup of flour and 1/2 cup of turkey stock; whisk until it makes a smooth paste.
Once it gets a golden brown color, add the rest of the stock and flour. Season with salt to taste. Let it simmer over medium heat, stirring constantly for 6 to 7 minutes.
Assemble the sandwiches with the turkey, gravy, tomato ketchup, mayonnaise, and pickles. Serve and enjoy!

# Pork

# Pork Pot Stickers

*(Ready in about 10 minutes | Servings 2)*

352 Calories; 13.5g Fat; 27.8g Carbs; 31.2g Protein; 2.2g Sugars

## Ingredients

1/2 pound lean ground pork
1/2 teaspoon fresh ginger, freshly grated
1 teaspoon chili garlic sauce
1 tablespoon soy sauce
1 tablespoon rice wine
1/4 teaspoon Szechuan pepper
2 stalks scallions, chopped
1 tablespoon sesame oil
8 (3-inch) round wonton wrappers

## Directions

Cook the ground pork in a preheated skillet until no longer pink,
crumbling with a fork. Stir in the other ingredients, except for the
wonton wrappers; stir to combine well.
Place the wonton wrappers on a clean work surface. Divide the pork
filling between the wrappers. Wet the edge of each wrapper with
water, fold the top half over the bottom half and pinch the border to
seal.
Place the pot stickers in the cooking basket and brush them with a
little bit of olive oil. Cook the pot sticker at 400 degrees F for 8
minutes. Serve immediately.

# Pork Shoulder with Molasses Sauce

*(Ready in about 25 minutes + marinating time | Servings 3)*

353 Calories; 19.6g Fat; 13.5g Carbs; 29.2g Protein; 12.2g Sugars

## *Ingredients*

2 tablespoons molasses

2 tablespoons soy sauce

2 tablespoons Shaoxing wine

2 garlic cloves, minced

1 teaspoon fresh ginger, minced

1 tablespoon cilantro stems and leaves, finely chopped

1 pound boneless pork shoulder

2 tablespoons sesame oil

## *Directions*

In a large-sized ceramic dish, thoroughly combine the molasses, soy sauce, wine, garlic, ginger, and cilantro; add the pork shoulder and allow it to marinate for 2 hours in the refrigerator.

Then, grease the cooking basket with sesame oil. Place the pork shoulder in the cooking basket; reserve the marinade.

Cook in the preheated Air Fryer at 395 degrees F for 14 to 17 minutes, flipping and basting with the marinade halfway through. Let it rest for 5 to 6 minutes before slicing and serving.

While the pork is roasting, cook the marinade in a preheated skillet over medium heat; cook until it has thickened.

Brush the pork shoulder with the sauce and enjoy!

# Sausage and Mushroom Chili

*(Ready in about 35 minutes | Servings 4)*

569 Calories; 35.3g Fat; 33.1g Carbs; 33.1g Protein; 10.4g Sugars

## Ingredients

1 tablespoon olive oil

1 shallot, chopped

2 garlic cloves, smashed

10 ounces button mushrooms, sliced

1/2 pound pork sausages, chopped

2 cups tomato puree

2 tablespoons tomato ketchup

1 teaspoon yellow mustard

1 cup chicken broth

2 teaspoons ancho chili powder

Salt and ground black pepper, to taste

1 (16-ounce) can pinto beans, rinsed and drained

1/2 cup cream cheese

## Directions

Start by preheating your Air Fryer to 360 degrees F. Heat the oil in a baking pan for a few minutes and cook the shallot until tender about 4 minutes.

Add the garlic and mushrooms; cook another 4 minutes or until tender and fragrant.

Next, stir in sausage and cook for a further 9 minutes. Add tomato puree, ketchup, mustard, and broth. Stir to combine and cook another 6 minutes.

Add spices and beans; cook an additional 7 minutes. Divide between individual bowls and top each bowl with cream cheese. Enjoy!

# Ribs with Cherry Tomatoes

*(Ready in about 35 minutes | Servings 2)*

452 Calories; 17.1g Fat; 17.7g Carbs; 55.2g Protein; 13.6g Sugars

## Ingredients

1 rack ribs, cut in half to fit the Air Fryer
1/4 cup dry white wine
2 tablespoons soy sauce
1 tablespoon Dijon mustard
Sea salt and ground black pepper, to taste
1 cup cherry tomatoes
1 teaspoon dried rosemary

## Directions

Toss the pork ribs with wine, soy sauce, mustard, salt, and black pepper.
Add the ribs to the lightly greased cooking basket. Cook in the preheated Air Fryer at 370 degrees F for 25 minutes.
Turn the ribs over, add the cherry tomatoes and rosemary; cook an additional 5 minutes. Serve immediately.

# Meatballs with Sweet and Sour Sauce

*(Ready in about 20 minutes | Servings 3)*

486 Calories; 14.8g Fat; 54.1g Carbs; 33.6g Protein; 20.4g Sugars

## Ingredients

Meatballs:
1/2 pound ground pork
1/4 pound ground turkey
1 tablespoons scallions, minced
1/2 teaspoon garlic, minced
4 tablespoons tortilla chips, crushed
4 tablespoons parmesan cheese, grated
1 egg, beaten
Salt and red pepper, to taste Sauce:
6 ounces jellied cranberry
2 ounces hot sauce
2 tablespoons molasses
1 tablespoon wine vinegar

## Directions

In a mixing bowl, thoroughly combine all ingredients for the meatballs. Stir to combine well and roll the mixture into 8 equal meatballs.
Cook in the preheated Air Fryer at 400 degrees F for 7 minutes. Shake the basket and continue to cook for 7 minutes longer.
Meanwhile, whisk the sauce ingredients in a nonstick skillet over low heat; let it simmer, partially covered, for about 20 minutes. Fold in the prepared meatballs and serve immediately.
Bon appétit!

# Beef

# Mayo Roasted Sirloin Steak

*(Ready in about 20 minutes | Servings 3)*

418 Calories; 31.3g Fat; 0.2g Carbs; 30.1g Protein; 0.2g Sugars

## Ingredients

1 pound sirloin steak, cubed

1/2 cup mayonnaise

1 tablespoon red wine vinegar

1/2 teaspoon dried basil

1 teaspoon garlic, minced

1/2 teaspoon cayenne pepper

Kosher salt and ground black pepper, to season

## Directions

Pat dry the sirloin steak with paper towels.

In a small mixing dish, thoroughly combine the remaining ingredients until everything is well incorporated.

Toss the cubed steak with the mayonnaise mixture and transfer to the Air Fryer cooking basket.

Cook in the preheated Air Fryer at 400 degrees F for 7 minutes. Shake the basket and continue to cook for a further 7 minutes. Bon appétit!

# Meatballs with Cranberry Sauce

*(Ready in about 40 minutes | Servings 4)*

520 Calories; 22.4g Fat; 44g Carbs; 45.4g Protein; 25.5g Sugars

## Ingredients

Meatballs:

1 ½ pounds ground chuck

1 egg

1 cup rolled oats

1/2 cup Romano cheese, grated

1/2 teaspoon dried basil

1/2 teaspoon dried oregano

1 teaspoon paprika

2 garlic cloves, minced

2 tablespoons scallions, chopped

Sea salt and cracked black pepper, to taste

**Cranberry Sauce:**

10 ounces BBQ sauce

8 ounces cranberry sauce

## Directions

In a large bowl, mix all ingredients for the meatballs. Mix until everything is well incorporated; then, shape the meat mixture into 2-inch balls using a cookie scoop. Transfer them to the lightly greased cooking basket and cook at 380 degrees F for 10 minutes. Shake the basket occasionally and work in batches. Add the BBQ sauce and cranberry sauce to a saucepan and cook over moderate heat until you achieve a glaze-like consistency; it will take about 15 minutes.

Gently stir in the air fried meatballs and cook an additional 3 minutes or until heated through. Enjoy

# Chuck Roast with Sweet 'n' Sticky Sauce

*(Ready in about 35 minutes | Servings 3)*

325 Calories; 16.8g Fat; 13.7g Carbs; 31.9g Protein; 12.8g Sugars

## Ingredients

1 pound chuck roast

Sea salt and ground black pepper, to taste

2 tablespoons butter, softened

1 tablespoon coriander, chopped

1 tablespoon fresh scallions, chopped

1 teaspoon soy sauce

1 tablespoon fish sauce

2 tablespoons honey

## Directions

Season the chuck roast with salt and pepper; spritz a nonstick cooking oil all over the beef.

Air fry at 400 degrees F for 30 to 35 minutes, flipping the chuck roast halfway through the cooking time.

While the roast is cooking, heat the other ingredients in a sauté pan over medium-high heat. Bring to a boil and reduce the heat; let it simmer, partially covered, until the sauce has thickened and reduced.

Slice the chuck roast into thick cuts and serve garnished with sweet 'n' sticky sauce. Bon appétit!

# Moroccan-Style Steak Salad

*(Ready in about 20 minutes | Servings 4)*

522 Calories; 21.7g Fat; 28.2g Carbs; 51.3g Protein; 13.5g Sugars

## Ingredients

1 pounds flank steak

1/4 cup soy sauce

4 tablespoons dry red wine

Salt, to taste

1/2 teaspoon ground black pepper

2 parsnips, peeled and sliced lengthways

1 teaspoon paprika

1 teaspoon onion powder

1 teaspoon garlic powder

1/2 teaspoon ground coriander

1/4 teaspoon ground allspice

2 tablespoons olive oil

2 tablespoons lime juice

1 teaspoon honey

1 cup lettuce leaves, shredded

1/2 cup pomegranate seeds

## *Directions*

Place the flank steak, soy sauce, wine, salt, and black pepper in a ceramic bowl. Let it marinate for 2 hours in your refrigerator. Transfer the meat to a lightly greased cooking basket. Top with parsnips. Add the paprika, onion powder, garlic powder, coriander, and allspice. Cook in the preheated Air Fryer at 400 degrees F for 7 minutes; turn over and cook an additional 5 minutes. In the meantime, make the dressing by mixing olive oil with lime juice and honey. Put the lettuce leaves and roasted parsnip in a salad bowl; toss with the dressing. Slice the steaks and place on top of the salad. Sprinkle over the pomegranate seeds and serve. Enjoy!

# Beef and Broccoli Stir-Fry

*(Ready in about 20 minutes | Servings 2)*

500 Calories; 23.1g Fat; 9.2g Carbs; 65g Protein; 2.4g Sugars

## Ingredients

1/2 pound beef stew meat, cut into bite-sized cubes
1/2 pound broccoli, cut into florets
1 small shallot, sliced
1 teaspoon peanut oil
1/2 teaspoon garlic powder
Salt and red pepper, to taste
1 teaspoon Five-spice powder
1 tablespoon fish sauce
1 tablespoon tamari sauce
1 teaspoon sesame seed oil
1 teaspoon Chiu Chow chili sauce

## Directions

Toss all ingredients until the beef and veggies are well coated.
Cook in the preheated Air Fryer at 400 degrees F for 6 minutes;
shake the basket and continue to air fry for 6 minutes more.
Now, test the meat for doneness, remove the vegetables and cook
the meat for 5 minutes more if needed.
Taste and adjust seasonings. Serve immediately.

# Fish

# Baked Sardines with Tangy Dipping Sauce

*(Ready in about 45 minutes | Servings 3)*

413 Calories; 29.1g Fat; 4g Carbs; 32g Protein; 1.7g Sugars

## Ingredients

1 pound fresh sardines
Sea salt and ground black pepper, to taste
1 teaspoon Italian seasoning mix
2 cloves garlic, minced
3 tablespoons olive oil
1/2 lemon, freshly squeezed

## Directions

Toss your sardines with salt, black pepper and Italian seasoning mix. Cook in your Air Fryer at 325 degrees F for 35 to 40 minutes until skin is crispy.
Meanwhile, make the sauce by whisking the remaining ingredients
Serve warm sardines with the sauce on the side. Bon appétit!

# Glazed Salmon Steaks

*(Ready in about 20 minutes | Servings 2)*

421 Calories; 16.8g Fat; 19.9g Carbs; 46.7g Protein; 18.1g Sugars

## Ingredients

1 salmon steaks
Coarse sea salt, to taste
1/4 teaspoon freshly ground black pepper, or more to taste
2 tablespoons honey
1 tablespoon sesame oil
Zest of 1 lemon
1 tablespoon fresh lemon juice
1 teaspoon garlic, minced
1/2 teaspoon smoked cayenne pepper
1/2 teaspoon dried dill

## Directions

Preheat your Air Fryer to 380 degrees F. Pat dry the salmon steaks
with a kitchen towel.
In a ceramic dish, combine the remaining ingredients until
everything is well whisked.
Add the salmon steaks to the ceramic dish and let them sit in the
refrigerator for 1 hour. Now, place the salmon steaks in the cooking
basket. Reserve the marinade.
Cook for 12 minutes, flipping halfway through the cooking time.
Meanwhile, cook the marinade in a small sauté pan over a moderate
flame. Cook until the sauce has thickened.
Pour the sauce over the steaks and serve with mashed potatoes if
desired. Bon appétit!

# Marinated Flounder Filets

*(Ready in about 15 minutes + marinating time | Servings 3)*

376 Calories; 14g Fat; 24.5g Carbs; 34.1g Protein; 4.8g Sugars

## Ingredients

1 pound flounder filets

1 teaspoon garlic, minced

2 tablespoons soy sauce

1 teaspoon Dijon mustard

1/4 cup malt vinegar

1 teaspoon granulated sugar

Salt and black pepper, to taste

1/2 cup plain flour

1 egg

2 tablespoons milk

1/2 cup parmesan cheese, grated

## Directions

Place the flounder filets, garlic, soy sauce, mustard, vinegar and sugar in a glass bowl; cover and let it marinate in your refrigerator for at least 1 hour. Transfer the fish to a plate, discarding the marinade. Salt and pepper to taste. Place the plain flour in a shallow bowl; in another bowl, beat the egg and milk until pale and well combined; add parmesan cheese to the third bowl. Dip the flounder filets in the flour, then in the egg mixture; repeat the process and coat them with the parmesan cheese, pressing to adhere.

Cook the flounder filets in the preheated Air Fryer at 400 degrees F for 5 minutes; turn the flounder filets over and cook on the other side for 5 minutes more. Enjoy!

# Tuna Steaks with Pearl Onions

*(Ready in about 20 minutes | Servings 4)*

332 Calories; 5.9g Fat; 10.5g Carbs; 56.1g Protein; 6.1g Sugars

## Ingredients

4 tuna steaks
1 pound pearl onions
4 teaspoons olive oil
1 teaspoon dried rosemary
1 teaspoon dried marjoram
1 tablespoon cayenne pepper
1/2 teaspoon sea salt
1/2 teaspoon black pepper, preferably freshly cracked
1 lemon, sliced

## Directions

Place the tuna steaks in the lightly greased cooking basket. Top with the pearl onions; add the olive oil, rosemary, marjoram, cayenne pepper, salt, and black pepper.
Bake in the preheated Air Fryer at 400 degrees F for 9 to 10 minutes. Work in two batches.
Serve warm with lemon slices and enjoy!

# Monkfish with Sautéed Vegetables and Olives

*(Ready in about 20 minutes | Servings 2)*

310 Calories; 13.3g Fat; 12.7g Carbs; 35.2g Protein; 5.4g Sugars

## Ingredients

2 teaspoons olive oil
2 carrots, sliced
2 bell peppers, sliced
1 teaspoon dried thyme
1/2 teaspoon dried marjoram
1/2 teaspoon dried rosemary
2 monkfish fillets
1 tablespoon soy sauce
2 tablespoons lime juice
Coarse salt and ground black pepper, to taste
1 teaspoon cayenne pepper
1/2 cup Kalamata olives, pitted and sliced

## Directions

In a nonstick skillet, heat the olive oil for 1 minute. Once hot, sauté the carrots and peppers until tender, about 4 minutes. Sprinkle with thyme, marjoram, and rosemary and set aside.

Toss the fish fillets with the soy sauce, lime juice, salt, black pepper, and cayenne pepper. Place the fish fillets in a lightly greased cooking basket and bake at 390 degrees F for 8 minutes.

Turn them over, add the olives, and cook an additional 4 minutes. Serve with the sautéed vegetables on the side. Bon appétit!

# Vegetable and Side Dishes

# Double-Cheese Stuffed Mushrooms

*(Ready in about 20 minutes | Servings 2)*

267 Calories; 19.6g Fat; 7.2g Carbs; 17.3g Protein; 2.9g Sugars

## Ingredients

8 medium-sized button mushrooms, stalks removed
1 teaspoon butter
1 teaspoon garlic, minced
Sea salt and ground black pepper, to taste
4 ounces Ricotta cheese, at room temperature
1/2 cup Romano cheese, grated
1/2 teaspoon ancho chili powder

## Directions

Clean your mushrooms and place them on a platter.
Then, mix the remaining ingredients in a bowl. Divide the filling
between your mushrooms and transfer them to a lightly greased
cooking basket.
Cook the mushrooms in the preheated Air Fryer at 380 degrees for
10 to 12 minutes. Serve warm and enjoy!

# Spicy Roasted Potatoes

*(Ready in about 15 minutes | Servings 2)*

299 Calories; 13.6g Fat; 40.9g Carbs; 4.8g Protein; 1.4g Sugars

## *Ingredients*

4 potatoes, peeled and cut into wedges
2 tablespoons olive oil
Sea salt and ground black pepper, to taste
1 teaspoon cayenne pepper
1/2 teaspoon ancho chili powder

## *Directions*

Toss all ingredients in a mixing bowl until the potatoes are well covered.
Transfer them to the Air Fryer basket and cook at 400 degrees F for 6 minutes; shake the basket and cook for a further 6 minutes.
Serve warm with your favorite sauce for dipping. Bon appétit!

# Baked Cauliflower

*(Ready in about 20 minutes | Servings 4)*

153 Calories; 7.3g Fat; 19.3g Carbs; 4.1g Protein; 2.9g Sugars

## Ingredients

1/2 cup all-purpose flour
1/2 cup water
Salt, to taste
1/2 teaspoon ground black pepper
1/2 teaspoon shallot powder
1/2 teaspoon garlic powder
1/2 teaspoon cayenne pepper
1 tablespoons olive oil
1 pound cauliflower, broken into small florets
1/4 cup Cholula sauce

## Directions

Start by preheating your Air Fryer to 400 degrees F. Lightly grease a baking pan with cooking spray.

In a mixing bowl, combine the flour, water, spices, and olive oil.

Coat the cauliflower with the prepared batter; arrange the cauliflower on the baking pan.

Then, bake in the preheated Air Fryer for 8 minutes or until golden brown.

Brush the Cholula sauce all over the cauliflower florets and bake an additional 4 to 5 minutes. Bon appétit!

# Mediterranean Vegetable Skewers

*(Ready in about 30 minutes | Servings 4)*

138 Calories; 10.2g Fat; 10.2g Carbs; 2.2g Protein; 6.6g Sugars

## Ingredients

1 medium-sized zucchini, cut into 1-inch pieces
2 red bell peppers, cut into 1-inch pieces
1 green bell pepper, cut into 1-inch pieces
1 red onion, cut into 1-inch pieces
2 tablespoons olive oil
Sea salt, to taste
1/2 teaspoon black pepper, preferably freshly cracked
1/2 teaspoon red pepper flakes

## Directions

Soak the wooden skewers in water for 15 minutes.
Thread the vegetables on skewers; drizzle olive oil all over the
vegetable skewers; sprinkle with spices.
Cook in the preheated Air Fryer at 400 degrees F for 13 minutes.
Serve warm and enjoy!

# Mediterranean-Style Roasted Broccoli

*(Ready in about 10 minutes | Servings 3)*

199 Calories; 15.6g Fat; 11.3g Carbs; 4.6g Protein; 2.8g Sugars

## Ingredients

1 pound broccoli florets
1 teaspoon butter, melted
Sea salt, to taste
1 teaspoon mixed peppercorns, crushed
1/4 cup mayonnaise
1 tablespoon fresh lemon juice
1 teaspoon deli mustard
2 cloves garlic, minced

## Directions

Toss the broccoli florets with butter, salt and crushed peppercorns until well coated on all sides.
Cook in the preheated Air Fryer at 400 degrees F for 6 minutes until they've softened.
In the meantime, make your aioli by mixing the mayo, lemon juice, mustard and garlic in a bowl.
Serve the roasted broccoli with the sauce on the side. Enjoy!

# SNACKS & APPETIZERS

# Parmesan Squash Chips

*(Ready in about 20 minutes | Servings 3)*

174 Calories; 6.1g Fat; 26.1g Carbs; 6.4g Protein; 9.3g Sugars

## Ingredients

3/4 pound butternut squash, cut into thin rounds
1/2 cup Parmesan cheese, grated
Sea salt and ground black pepper, to taste
1 teaspoon butter
1/2 cup ketchup
1 teaspoon Sriracha sauce

## Directions

Toss the butternut squash with Parmesan cheese, salt, black pepper and butter.
Transfer the butternut squash rounds to the Air Fryer cooking basket.
Air Fryer at 400 degrees F for 12 minutes. Shake the Air Fryer basket periodically to ensure even cooking. Work with batches.
While the parmesan squash chips are baking, whisk the ketchup and sriracha and set it aside.
Serve the parmesan squash chips with Sriracha ketchup and enjoy!

# Chili-Lime French Fries

*(Ready in about 20 minutes | Servings 3)*

128 Calories; 1.9g Fat; 26.6g Carbs; 2.8g Protein; 2.2g Sugars

## Ingredients

1 pound potatoes, peeled and cut into matchsticks
1 teaspoon olive oil
1 lime, freshly squeezed
1 teaspoon chili powder
Sea salt and ground black pepper, to taste

## Directions

Toss your potatoes with the remaining ingredients until well coated.
Transfer your potatoes to the Air Fryer cooking basket.
Cook the French fries at 370 degrees F for 9 minutes. Shake the
cooking basket and continue to cook for about 9 minutes. Serve
immediately. Bon appétit!

# Meatball Skewers

*(Ready in about 20 minutes | Servings 6)*

218 Calories; 13g Fat; 10.7g Carbs; 14.1g Protein; 8.5g Sugars

## Ingredients

1/2 pound ground pork
1/2 pound ground beef
1 teaspoon dried onion flakes
1 teaspoon fresh garlic, minced
1 teaspoon dried parsley flakes
Salt and black pepper, to taste
1 red pepper, 1-inch pieces
1 cup pearl onions
1/2 cup barbecue sauce

## Directions

Mix the ground meat with the onion flakes, garlic, parsley flakes, salt, and black pepper. Shape the mixture into 1-inch balls.
Thread the meatballs, pearl onions, and peppers alternately onto skewers.
Microwave the barbecue sauce for 10 seconds.
Cook in the preheated Air Fryer at 380 degrees for 5 minutes. Turn the skewers over halfway through the cooking time. Brush with the sauce and cook for a further 5 minutes. Work in batches.
Serve with the remaining barbecue sauce and enjoy!

# Asian Chicken Wings

*(Ready in about 20 minutes | Servings 6)*

195 Calories; 5.7g Fat; 9.4g Carbs; 25.5g Protein; 6.4g Sugars

## Ingredients

1 ½ pounds chicken wings

2 teaspoons sesame oil

Kosher salt and ground black pepper, to taste

2 tablespoons tamari sauce

1 tablespoon rice vinegar

2 garlic clove, minced

2 tablespoons honey

2 sun-dried tomatoes, minced

## Directions

Toss the chicken wings with the sesame oil, salt, and pepper. Add chicken wings to a lightly greased baking pan.

Roast the chicken wings in the preheated Air Fryer at 390 degrees F for 7 minutes. Turn them over once or twice to ensure even cooking. In a mixing dish, thoroughly combine the tamari sauce, vinegar, garlic, honey, and sun-dried tomatoes.

Pour the sauce all over the chicken wings; bake an additional 5 minutes. Bon appétit!

# Sweet Potato Chips with Chili Mayo

*(Ready in about 35 minutes | Servings 3)*

218 Calories; 19.6g Fat; 9.5g Carbs; 1g Protein; 1.9g Sugars

## Ingredients

1 sweet potato, cut into 1/8-inch-thick slices
1 teaspoon olive oil
Sea salt and cracked mixed peppercorns, to taste
1/2 teaspoon turmeric powder
1/3 cup mayonnaise
1 teaspoon granulated garlic
1/2 teaspoon red chili flakes

## Directions

Toss the sweet potato slices with olive oil, salt, cracked peppercorns and turmeric powder.

Cook your sweet potatoes at 380 degrees F for 33 to 35 minutes, tossing the basket every 10 minutes to ensure even cooking. Work with batches.

Meanwhile, mix the mayonnaise, garlic and red chili flakes to make the sauce.

The sweet potato chips will crisp up as it cools. Serve the sweet potato chips with the chili mayo on the side.

# Rice and Grains

# Mexicana Air Grilled Fish Tacos

*(Ready in about 15 minutes | Servings 3)*

422 Calories; 11.5g Fat; 41.3g Carbs; 39g Protein; 3.3g Sugars

## Ingredients

1 pound tilapia filets
1 teaspoon chipotle powder
1 teaspoon fresh coriander, finely chopped
1 teaspoon fresh garlic, minced
1 teaspoon extra-virgin olive oil
1 teaspoon taco seasoning mix
1 cup pickled cabbage, drained and shredded
6 mini taco shells

## Directions

Toss the tilapia filets with the chipotle powder, coriander, garlic, olive oil and taco seasoning mix.

Cook the fish in your Air Fryer at 400 degrees F for 10 minutes, flipping halfway through the cooking time.

Remove the tilapia filets to a cutting board then flake into pieces.

To assemble the tacos, divide the fish and pickled cabbage between taco shells. Roll them up and transfer to the Air Fryer cooking basket.

Bake your tacos at 360 degrees F for 5 minutes until thoroughly warmed. Bon appétit!

# Mediterranean Monkey Bread

*(Ready in about 20 minutes | Servings 6)*

427 Calories; 25.4g Fat; 38.1g Carbs; 11.6g Protein; 6.5g Sugars

## Ingredients

1 (16-ounce) can refrigerated buttermilk biscuits
3 tablespoons olive oil
1 cup Provolone cheese, grated
1/4 cup black olives, pitted and chopped
4 tablespoons basil pesto
1/4 cup pine nuts, chopped
1 tablespoon Mediterranean herb mix

## Directions

Separate your dough into the biscuits and cut each of them in half;
roll them into balls. Dip each ball into the olive oil and begin layering
in a nonstick Bundt pan.
Cover the bottom of the pan with one layer of dough balls.
Prepare the coating mixtures. In a shallow bowl, place the provolone
cheese and olives, add the basil pesto to a second bowl and add the
pine nuts to a third bowl.
Roll the dough balls in the coating mixtures; then, arrange them in
the Bundt pan so the various coatings are alternated. Top with
Mediterranean herb mix
Cook the monkey bread in the Air Fryer at 320 degrees for 13 to 16
minutes. Bon appétit!

# Fish Tacos

*(Ready in about 25 minutes | Servings 3)*

493 Calories; 19.2g Fat; 48.4g Carbs; 30.8g Protein; 5.8g Sugars

## *Ingredients*

1 tablespoon mayonnaise
1 teaspoon Dijon mustard
1 tablespoon sour cream
1/2 teaspoon fresh garlic, minced
1/4 teaspoon red pepper flakes
Sea salt, to taste
2 bell peppers, seeded and sliced
1 shallot, thinly sliced
1 egg
1 tablespoon water
1 tablespoon taco seasoning mix
1/3 cup tortilla chips, crushed
1/4 cup parmesan cheese, grated
1 halibut fillets, cut into 1-inch strips
6 mini flour taco shells
6 lime wedges, for serving

### Directions

Thoroughly combine the mayonnaise, mustard, sour cream, garlic, red pepper flakes, and salt. Add the bell peppers and shallots; toss to coat well. Place in your refrigerator until ready to serve.

Line the Air Fryer basket with a piece of parchment paper.

In a shallow bowl, mix the egg, water, and taco seasoning mix. In a separate shallow bowl, mix the crushed tortilla chips and parmesan.

Dip the fish into the egg mixture, then coat with the parmesan mixture, pressing to adhere.

Bake in the preheated Air Fryer at 380 degrees F for 13 minutes, flipping halfway through the cooking time.

Divide the creamed pepper mixture among the taco shells. Top with the fish, and serve with lime wedges. Enjoy!

# Greek Tiganites

*(Ready in about 50 minutes | Servings 3)*

384 Calories; 14.1g Fat; 55.2g Carbs; 11.8g Protein; 20.5g Sugars

## Ingredients

1/2 cup plain flour
1/2 cup barley flour
1 teaspoon baking powder
A pinch of salt
A pinch of sugar
A pinch of cinnamon
1 egg
1/2 cup milk
1/2 cup carbonated water
1 tablespoon butter, melted
3 tablespoons honey
3 tablespoons walnuts, chopped
3 tablespoons Greek yogurt

## Directions

Thoroughly combine the flour, baking powder, salt, sugar and cinnamon in a large bowl. Fold in the egg and mix again.
Gradually pour in the milk, water and melted butter, whisking continuously, until well combined. Let the batter stand for about 30 minutes. Spritz the Air Fryer baking pan with a cooking spray. Pour the batter into the pan using a measuring cup.
Cook at 230 degrees F for 6 to 8 minutes or until golden brown. Repeat with the remaining batter.
Serve your tiganites with the honey, walnuts and Greek yogurt. Enjoy!

# Air Fryer Cornbread

*(Ready in about 30 minutes | Servings 4)*

455 Calories; 23.9g Fat; 46.1g Carbs; 13.9g Protein; 4.7g Sugars

## Ingredients

3/4 cup cornmeal

1 cup flour

2 teaspoons baking powder

1/2 tablespoon brown sugar

1/2 teaspoon salt

5 tablespoons butter, melted

3 eggs, beaten

1 cup full-fat milk

## Directions

Start by preheating your Air Fryer to 370 degrees F. Then, spritz a baking pan with cooking oil.

In a mixing bowl, combine the flour, cornmeal, baking powder, brown sugar, and salt. In a separate bowl, mix the butter, eggs, and milk.

Pour the egg mixture into the dry cornmeal mixture; mix to combine well.

Pour the batter into the baking pan; cover with aluminum foil and poke tiny little holes all over the foil. Now, bake for 15 minutes. Remove the foil and bake for 10 minutes more. Transfer to a wire rack to cool slightly before cutting and serving. Bon appétit

# Vegan

# Italian-Style Tomato Cutlets

*(Ready in about 10 minutes | Servings 2)*

181 Calories; 2.6g Fat; 32.2g Carbs; 6.1g Protein; 4.1g Sugars

## Ingredients

1 beefsteak tomato – sliced into halves
1/2 cup all-purpose flour
1/2 cup almond milk
1/2 cup breadcrumbs
1 teaspoon Italian seasoning mix

## Directions

Pat the beefsteak tomato dry and set it aside.

In a shallow bowl, mix the all-purpose flour with almond milk. In another bowl, mix breadcrumbs with Italian seasoning mix.

Dip the beefsteak tomatoes in the flour mixture; then, coat the beefsteak tomatoes with the breadcrumb mixture, pressing to adhere to both sides.

Cook your tomatoes at 360 degrees F for about 5 minutes; turn them over and cook on the other side for 5 minutes longer. Serve at room temperature and enjoy!

# Crispy Butternut Squash Fries

*(Ready in about 25 minutes | Servings 4)*

288 Calories; 7.6g Fat; 45.6g Carbs; 11.4g Protein; 3.1g Sugars

## Ingredients

1 cup all-purpose flour
Salt and ground black pepper, to taste
3 tablespoons nutritional yeast flakes
1/2 cup almond milk
1/2 cup almond meal
1/2 cup bread crumbs
1 tablespoon herbs (oregano, basil, rosemary), chopped
1 pound butternut squash, peeled and cut into French fry shapes

## Directions

In a shallow bowl, combine the flour, salt, and black pepper. In another shallow dish, mix the nutritional yeast flakes with the almond milk until well combined.

Mix the almond meal, breadcrumbs, and herbs in a third shallow dish. Dredge the butternut squash in the flour mixture, shaking off the excess. Then, dip in the milk mixture; lastly, dredge in the breadcrumb mixture.

Spritz the butternut squash fries with cooking oil on all sides. Cook in the preheated Air Fryer at 400 degrees F approximately 12 minutes, turning them over halfway through the cooking time. Serve with your favorite sauce for dipping. Bon appétit!

# Granola with Raisins and Nuts

*(Ready in about 40 minutes | Servings 8)*

222 Calories; 14g Fat; 29.9g Carbs; 5.3g Protein; 11.3g Sugars

## *Ingredients*

2 cups rolled oats
1/2 cup walnuts, chopped
1/3 cup almonds chopped
1/4 cup raisins
1/4 cup whole wheat pastry flour
1/2 teaspoon cinnamon
1/4 teaspoon nutmeg, preferably freshly grated
1/2 teaspoon salt
1/3 cup coconut oil, melted
1/3 cup agave nectar
1/2 teaspoon coconut extract
1/2 teaspoon vanilla extract

## *Directions*

Thoroughly combine all ingredients. Then, spread the mixture onto the Air Fryer trays. Spritz with cooking spray.
Bake at 230 degrees F for 25 minutes; rotate the trays and bake 10 to 15 minutes more.
This granola can be stored in an airtight container for up to 2 weeks. Enjoy!

# Corn on the Cob with Spicy Avocado Spread

*(Ready in about 15 minutes | Servings 4)*

234 Calories; 9.2g Fat; 37.9g Carbs; 7.2g Protein; 1.9g Sugars

## Ingredients

4 corn cobs
1 avocado, pitted, peeled and mashed
1 clove garlic, pressed
1 tablespoon fresh lime juice
1 tablespoon soy sauce
4 teaspoons nutritional yeast
1/2 teaspoon cayenne pepper
1/2 teaspoon dried dill
Sea salt and ground black pepper, to taste
1 teaspoon hot sauce
2 heaping tablespoons fresh cilantro leaves, roughly chopped

## Directions

Spritz the corn with cooking spray. Cook at 390 degrees F for 6 minutes, turning them over halfway through the cooking time.
In the meantime, mix the avocado, lime juice, soy sauce, nutritional yeast, cayenne pepper, dill, salt, black pepper, and hot sauce.
Spread the avocado mixture all over the corn on the cob. Garnish with fresh cilantro leaves. Bon appétit!

# Corn on the Cob with Mediterranean Sauce

*(Ready in about 10 minutes | Servings 2)*

434 Calories; 27.4g Fat; 45.1g Carbs; 10.8g Protein; 5.4g Sugars

## Ingredients

2 ears corn, husked

1/3 cup raw cashews, soaked

2 cloves garlic, minced

1/2 teaspoon nutritional yeast

1/2 teaspoon Dijon mustard

4 tablespoons oat milk

1 tablespoon extra-virgin olive oil

1 teaspoon freshly squeezed lemon juice

Sea salt and ground black pepper, to taste

## Directions

Cook your corn in the preheated Air Fryer at 390 degrees F for about 6 minutes.

Meanwhile, blitz the remaining ingredients in your food processor or blender until smooth, creamy and uniform.

Rub each ear of corn with the Mediterranean spread and serve immediately. Bon appétit!

# Dessert

# Cake with Walnuts

*(Ready in about 20 minutes | Servings 4)*

455 Calories; 25.4g Fat; 52.1g Carbs; 6.1g Protein; 15g Sugars

## Ingredients

1 (10-ounces) can crescent rolls
1/2 stick butter
1/2 cup caster sugar
1 teaspoon pumpkin pie spice blend
1 tablespoon dark rum
1/2 cup walnuts, chopped

## Directions

Start by preheating your Air Fryer to 350 degrees F.
Roll out the crescent rolls. Spread the butter onto the crescent rolls; scatter the sugar, spices and walnuts over the rolls. Drizzle with rum and roll them up.
Using your fingertips, gently press them to seal the edges.
Bake your cake for about 13 minutes or until the top is golden brown. Bon appétit!

# Fruit Kabobs

*(Ready in about 10 minutes | Servings 6)*

165 Calories; 0.7g Fat; 41.8g Carbs; 1.6g Protein; 33.6g Sugars

## Ingredients

2 pears, diced into bite-sized chunks
2 apples, diced into bite-sized chunks
2 mangos, diced into bite-sized chunks
1 tablespoon fresh lemon juice
1 teaspoon vanilla essence
2 tablespoons maple syrup
1 teaspoon ground cinnamon
1/2 teaspoon ground cloves

## Directions

Toss all ingredients in a mixing dish.
Tread the fruit pieces on skewers.
Cook at 350 degrees F for 5 minutes. Bon appétit!

# Cinnamon Dough Dippers

*(Ready in about 20 minutes | Servings 6)*

332 Calories; 14.8g Fat; 45.6g Carbs; 5.1g Protein; 27.6g Sugars

## Ingredients

1/2 pound bread dough
1/4 cup butter, melted
1/2 cup caster sugar
1 tablespoon cinnamon
1/2 cup cream cheese, softened
1 cup powdered sugar
1/2 teaspoon vanilla
2 tablespoons milk

## Directions

Roll the dough into a log; cut into 1-1/2 inch strips using a pizza cutter.

Mix the butter, sugar, and cinnamon in a small bowl. Use a rubber spatula to spread the butter mixture over the tops of the dough dippers.

Bake at 360 degrees F for 7 to 8 minutes, turning them over halfway through the cooking time. Work in batches.

Meanwhile, make the glaze dip by whisking the remaining ingredients with a hand mixer. Beat until a smooth consistency is reached.

Serve at room temperature and enjoy!

# Sweet Dough Dippers

*(Ready in about 10 minutes | Servings 4)*

255 Calories; 7.6g Fat; 42.1g Carbs; 5g Protein; 17.1g Sugars

## Ingredients

8 ounces bread dough

2 tablespoons butter, melted

2 ounces powdered sugar

## Directions

Cut the dough into strips and twist them together 3 to 4 times. Then, brush the dough twists with melted butter and sprinkle sugar over them.

Cook the dough twists at 350 degrees F for 8 minutes, tossing the basket halfway through the cooking time.

Serve with your favorite dip. Bon appétit!

# Banana Chips with Chocolate Glaze

*(Ready in about 20 minutes | Servings 2)*

201 Calories; 7.5g Fat; 37.1g Carbs; 1.8g Protein; 22.9g Sugars

## Ingredients

2 banana, cut into slices
1/4 teaspoon lemon zest
1 tablespoon agave syrup
1 tablespoon cocoa powder
1 tablespoon coconut oil, melted

## Directions

Toss the bananas with the lemon zest and agave syrup. Transfer your bananas to the parchmentlined cooking basket.

Bake in the preheated Air Fryer at 370 degrees F for 12 minutes, turning them over halfway through the cooking time.

In the meantime, melt the coconut oil in your microwave; add the cocoa powder and whisk to combine well.

Serve the baked banana chips with a few drizzles of the chocolate glaze. Enjoy!

# Other Air Fryer Recipes

# Chicken and Peppers

*(Ready in about 45 minutes | Servings 3)*

397 Calories; 18.8g Fat; 20.6g Carbs; 34.2g Protein; 3.1g Sugars

## Ingredients

1/2 cup all-purpose four
1 teaspoon kosher salt
1 teaspoon shallot powder
1/2 teaspoon dried basil
1/2 teaspoon dried oregano
1/2 teaspoon smoked paprika
1 tablespoon hot sauce
1/4 cup mayonnaise
1/4 cup milk
1 pound chicken drumettes
1 bell peppers, sliced

## Directions

In a shallow bowl, mix the flour, salt, shallot powder, basil, oregano and smoked paprika.
In another bowl, mix the hot sauce, mayonnaise and milk.
Dip the chicken drumettes in the flour mixture, then, coat them with the milk mixture; make sure to coat well on all sides.
Cook in the preheated Air Fryer at 380 degrees F for 28 to 30 minutes; turn them over halfway through the cooking time. Reserve chicken drumettes, keeping them warm.
Then, cook the peppers at 400 degrees F for 13 to 15 minutes, shaking the basket once or twice.

# Pork with Brussels sprouts

*(Ready in about 20 minutes | Servings 3)*

381 Calories; 11.7g Fat; 14.1g Carbs; 56g Protein; 3.4g Sugars

## *Ingredients*

1 pound Brussels sprouts, halved
1 ½ pounds tenderloin
1 teaspoon peanut oil
1 teaspoon garlic powder
1 tablespoon coriander, minced
1 teaspoon smoked paprika
Sea salt and ground black pepper, to taste

## Directions

Toss the Brussels sprouts and pork with oil and spices until well coated.
Place in the Air Fryer cooking basket. Cook in the preheated Air Fryer at 370 degrees F for 15 minutes.
Taste and adjust seasonings. Eat warm.

# Greek Style Roast Beef

*(Ready in about 55 minutes | Servings 3)*

348 Calories; 16.1g Fat; 1.6g Carbs; 49g Protein; 0.9g Sugars

## Ingredients

1 clove garlic, halved
1 ½ pounds beef eye round roast
1 zucchini, sliced lengthwise
2 teaspoons olive oil
1 teaspoon Greek spice mix
Sea salt, to season
1/2 cup Greek-style yogurt

## Directions

Rub the beef eye round roast with garlic halves.
Brush the beef eye round roast and zucchini with olive oil. Sprinkle with spices and place the beef in the cooking basket.
Roast in your Air Fryer at 400 degrees F for 40 minutes. Turn the beef over.
Add the zucchini to the cooking basket and continue to cook for 12 minutes more or until cooked through. Serve warm, garnished with Greek-style yogurt.

# Squid with Southern Flavors

*(Ready in about 10 minutes | Servings 2)*

529 Calories; 24.3g Fat; 41g Carbs; 33.2g Protein; 3.2g Sugar

## Ingredients

1/2 pound calamari tubes cut into rings, cleaned
Sea salt and ground black pepper, to season
1/2 cup almond flour
1/2 cup all-purpose flour
4 tablespoons parmesan cheese, grated
1/2 cup ale beer
1/4 teaspoon cayenne pepper
1/2 cup breadcrumbs
1/4 cup mayonnaise
1/4 cup Greek-style yogurt
1 clove garlic, minced
1 tablespoon fresh lemon juice
1 teaspoon fresh parsley, chopped
1 teaspoon fresh dill, chopped

## *Directions*

Sprinkle the calamari with salt and black pepper.

Mix the flour, cheese and beer in a bowl until well combined. In another bowl, mix cayenne pepper and breadcrumbs

Dip the calamari pieces in the flour mixture, then roll them onto the breadcrumb mixture, pressing to coat on all sides; transfer them to a lightly oiled cooking basket.

Cook at 400 degrees F for 4 minutes, shaking the basket halfway through the cooking time.

Meanwhile, mix the remaining ingredients until everything is well incorporated. Serve warm calamari with the sauce for dipping.

# Roasted Squash

*(Ready in about 15 minutes | Servings 3)*

189 Calories; 8.4g Fat; 22.3g Carbs; 6.7g Protein; 5.8g Sugars

## *Ingredients*

1 pound acorn squash, peeled, seeded and cubed
1 teaspoon coconut oil, melted
1 tablespoon honey
1/4 teaspoon grated nutmeg
1/4 teaspoon ground cloves
1/2 teaspoon cinnamon powder
1/4 teaspoon ground white pepper
1/2 teaspoon dread dill weed
1/2 cup chèvre cheese, crumbled

## *Directions*

Toss the acorn squash cubes with coconut oil, honey, nutmeg, cloves, cinnamon, white pepper and dill weed.
Transfer the acorn squash to a lightly greased cooking basket.
Cook the acorn squash in the preheated Air Fryer at 400 degrees F for 6 minutes; shake the basket and cook for a further 6 minutes.
Place the roasted squash on a serving platter, garnish with chèvre cheese and serve.

# Pear in Chips with Cinnamon

*(Ready in about 10 minutes | Servings 2)*

94 Calories; 2.6g Fat; 18.1g Carbs; 0.7g Protein; 12.6g Sugars

## Ingredients

1 large pear, cored and sliced
1 teaspoon apple pie spice blend
1 teaspoon coconut oil
1 teaspoon honey

## Directions

Toss the pear slices with the spice blend, coconut oil and honey.
Then, place the pear slices in the Air Fryer cooking basket and cook
at 360 degrees F for about 8 minutes.
Shake the basket once or twice to ensure even cooking. Pear chips
will crisp up as it cools.

# Mac and Cheese

*(Ready in about 25 minutes | Servings 2)*

439 Calories; 24.4g Fat; 34.4g Carbs; 19.5g Protein; 3.6g Sugars

## Ingredients

3/4 cup cavatappi
1/4 cup double cream
4 ounces Colby cheese, shredded
1/2 teaspoon granulated garlic
Sea salt and ground black pepper, to taste
1/4 teaspoon cayenne pepper

## Directions

Bring a pot of salted water to a boil over high heat; turn the heat down to medium and add the cavatappi.
Let it simmer about 8 minutes. Drain cavatappi, reserving 1/4 cup of the cooking water; add them to a lightly greased baking pan.
Add in 1/4 cup of the cooking water, double cream, cheese and spices to the baking pan; gently stir to combine.
Bake your mac and cheese in the preheated Air Fryer at 360 degrees F for 15 minutes. Garnish with fresh basil leaves if desired.

# Australian Style Pancakes

*(Ready in about 30 minutes | Servings 4)*

370 Calories; 5.8g Fat; 72.3g Carbs; 10.2g Protein; 48.2g Sugars

## Ingredients

1/2 cup flour
A pinch of salt
A pinch of sugar
1/2 cup whole milk
3 eggs
1 shot of rum
4 tablespoons raisins
1/2 cup icing sugar
1/2 cup stewed plums

## Directions

Mix the flour, salt, sugar, and milk in a bowl until the batter becomes semi-solid.

Fold in the eggs; add the rum and whisk to combine well. Let it stand for 20 minutes.

Spritz the Air Fryer baking pan with cooking spray. Pour the batter into the pan using a measuring cup. Scatter the raisins over the top. Cook at 230 degrees F for 4 to 5 minutes or until golden brown. Repeat with the remaining batter.

Cut the pancake into pieces, sprinkle over the icing sugar, and serve with the stewed plums.

# Blueberry Pancakes with Raw Sugar

*(Ready in about 20 minutes | Servings 4)*

218 Calories; 6.6g Fat; 35.6g Carbs; 4.7g Protein; 22.5g Sugars

## Ingredients

1/2 cup plain flour
1/2 teaspoon baking powder
1 teaspoon brown sugar
A pinch of grated nutmeg
1/4 teaspoon ground star anise
A pinch of salt
1 egg
1/4 cup coconut milk
1 cup fresh blueberries
1 tablespoon coconut oil, melted
4 tablespoons cinnamon sugar

## Directions

Combine the flour, baking powder, brown sugar, nutmeg, star anise and salt. In another bowl, whisk the eggs and milk until frothy. Add the wet mixture to the dry mixture and mix to combine well. Fold in the fresh blueberries. Carefully place spoonfuls of batter into the Air Fryer cooking basket. Brush them with melted coconut oil.
Cook your fritters in the preheated Air Fryer at 370 degrees for 10 minutes, flipping them halfway through the cooking time. Repeat with the remaining batter.
Dust your fritters with the cinnamon sugar and serve at room temperature.

SAM HAMIL

CPSIA information can be obtained
at www.ICGtesting.com
Printed in the USA
BVHW091408290621
610728BV00004B/1192

9 781802 751413